APHRODITE

GREEK GODDESS OF LOVE AND BEAUTY

by Tammy Gagne

Content Consultant
Susan C. Shelmerdine, PhD,
Professor of Classical Studies
University of North Carolina, Greensboro
Greensboro, NC

CAPSTONE PRESS
a capstone imprint

Snap Books are published by Capstone Press,
1710 Roe Crest Drive, North Mankato, Minnesota 56003
www.mycapstone.com

Library of Congress Cataloging-in-Publication Data
Names: Gagne, Tammy, author.
Title: Aphrodite: Greek goddess of love and beauty / by Tammy Gagne
Description: North Mankato : Capstone Press, 2019. | Series: Snap Books.
   Legendary goddesses | Includes index.
Identifiers: LCCN 2018036724| ISBN 9781543554519 (library binding) |
   ISBN 9781543559149 (pbk.) | ISBN 9781543554557 (ebook pdf)
Subjects: LCSH: Aphrodite (Greek deity)—Juvenile literature.
Classification: LCC BL820.V5 G34 2019 | DDC 292.2/114—dc23
LC record available at https://lccn.loc.gov/2018036724

Editorial Credits
Gina Kammer, editor
Bobbie Nuytten, designer
Svetlana Zhurkin, media researcher
Katy LaVigne, production specialist

Image Credits
Alamy: Chronicle, 7, Prisma Archivo, cover, Science History Images, 29
(top); Bridgeman Images: Museum of Fine Arts, Houston, Texas, USA/Gift
of Miss Annette Finnigan/Victoriatus with Zeus and Dione on obverse and
thunderbolt in wreath with legend on reverse, 238-168 BC (silver), Greek
School, (3rd-2nd century BC), 12; Getty Images: DEA/A. Dagli Orti, 14,
DEA/G. Dagli Orti, 5, Mondadori Portfolio, 25 (bottom left); Newscom:
akg-images, 8, 22, 27 (bottom), 29 (bottom), Album/Fine Art Images, 16,
27 (top), Heritage Images/Art Media, 9 (top), Heritage Images/London
Metropolitan Archives/City of London, 20, Heritage Images/The Print
Collector, 21; Shutterstock: Debu55y, 28, Elena Efimova, 4, EleniKa, 25 (top),
Gala_Kan, 17, John_Silver, 24, LeniKovaleva, 10, leoks, 26, Maksimilian, 11,
Mark Lijesen, 15, Masterrr, 18, 19, Sanit Fuangnakhon, 9 (bottom), Stavrida,
25 (bottom right), Yakov Oskanov, 13

Design Elements by Shutterstock

Printed and bound in the USA.
PA49

TABLE OF CONTENTS

Chapter 1

TO THE FAIREST

Aphrodite was the Greek goddess of love and beauty. One of the main myths about Aphrodite takes place during a celebration of love, which she attended. A joyous event was about to take place on Mount Pelion. King Peleus was marrying a sea **nymph** named Thetis. All the Greek gods and goddesses were invited to the wedding except Eris, the goddess of **discord**. She became furious when she found out and decided to get revenge by causing trouble. So she tossed a golden apple into the crowd. On the fruit she had written the words, "To the Fairest."

Three goddesses claimed the gift. Hera was the wife of Zeus and queen of all the gods and goddesses. She was sure the apple was meant for her. Athena was the goddess of wisdom. She knew that no one was more beautiful than she was. She could not imagine that the gift could be for anyone but her. But Aphrodite was the goddess of love. She was a great beauty, herself. She too claimed the apple and the title of the fairest.

The three beautiful goddesses, Hera, Athena, and Aphrodite, await judgement by Paris to find out who is fairest among them.

Eris had accomplished her goal. The guests were not focused on the happy couple. Instead, they could not stop watching the fight for the golden apple. When the three goddesses couldn't work it out themselves, they turned to Zeus. But the king of all the gods wanted nothing to do with the decision. He did not want to be the one to anger two of the women in his family by choosing only one of the three. He turned the decision over to Paris, a **mortal** prince of Troy.

nymph—a minor female goddess who lives on earth
discord—lack of agreement; conflict
mortal—human, referring to a being who will eventually die

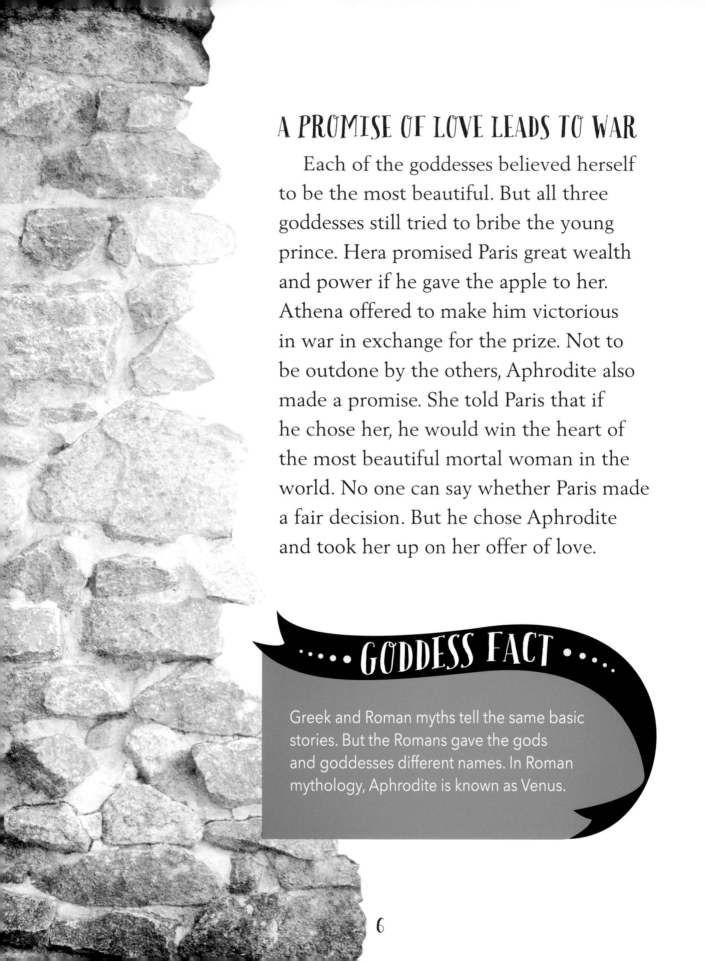

A PROMISE OF LOVE LEADS TO WAR

Each of the goddesses believed herself to be the most beautiful. But all three goddesses still tried to bribe the young prince. Hera promised Paris great wealth and power if he gave the apple to her. Athena offered to make him victorious in war in exchange for the prize. Not to be outdone by the others, Aphrodite also made a promise. She told Paris that if he chose her, he would win the heart of the most beautiful mortal woman in the world. No one can say whether Paris made a fair decision. But he chose Aphrodite and took her up on her offer of love.

GODDESS FACT

Greek and Roman myths tell the same basic stories. But the Romans gave the gods and goddesses different names. In Roman mythology, Aphrodite is known as Venus.

When Paris chose between the goddesses, he was living as a shepherd and did not yet know that he was a prince.

To Paris, the most beautiful woman was Helen, the wife of the Spartan King Menelaus. Aphrodite helped the prince hatch a plan to kidnap the young queen so they could run away together. Menelaus responded by sending more than 1,000 ships to find his wife and bring her back. Under Aphrodite's influence, Paris's decisions led the people of Greece and Troy into the Trojan War.

Helen was taken away from Sparta to be with Paris.

The Goddess of Love and Beauty

In addition to being the goddess of love, Aphrodite was also the goddess of beauty. Many people of ancient Greece worshipped her. They hoped to be rewarded with great love of their own. Women thought worshipping Aphrodite would bring them children.

Aphrodite was also worshipped as a sea goddess. Sailors believed that she brought calm waters and safe travels. For this reason they often prayed to her before their voyages.

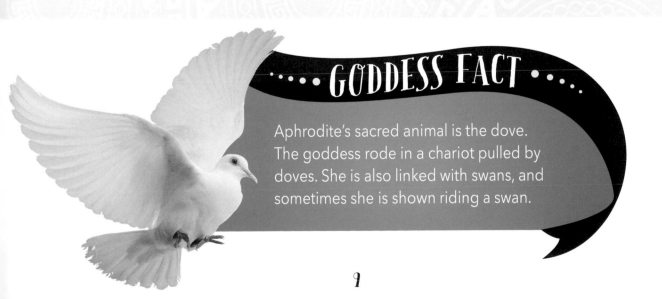

GODDESS FACT

Aphrodite's sacred animal is the dove. The goddess rode in a chariot pulled by doves. She is also linked with swans, and sometimes she is shown riding a swan.

Chapter 2

THE CREATION OF APHRODITE

Myths like the story of the golden apple were important to the ancient Greeks. They believed that gods and goddesses controlled the world from the top of Mount Olympus. The oldest myths about Aphrodite say her father was Uranus, god of the sky. In these stories, Aphrodite has no mother. She is born from the foam of the sea as a fully formed adult. This all takes place two **generations** before Zeus himself is born. Then Uranus ruled the universe with his wife Gaia, the Earth goddess.

Aphrodite never knew her father. Uranus had other children before Aphrodite. But he did not love any of them. In fact, he hated them so much that he hid his oldest children away deep in the Earth. But Gaia wanted to free them. She gave her son Cronus a **sickle**. When Cronus attacked Uranus with this weapon, parts of his body fell into the ocean and became the foam from which Aphrodite was born.

Aphrodite is often shown rising from a shell, which symbolizes how she was born from the sea.

The ancient Greek poet Hesiod told this creation story about Aphrodite around 700 BC. According to Hesiod, Aphrodite floated past the island of Cytherea as foam. And she kept floating until she came to Cyprus. Once there, she walked ashore as a goddess. The ancient Greeks built a **temple** to honor Aphrodite on this island in the Mediterranean Sea. People throughout Greece worshipped Aphrodite.

generation—a group of people born around the same time
sickle—a long, curved blade attached to a short handle
temple—a building used for worship

····· GODDESS FACT ·····

Aphrodite's name comes from the Greek word *aphros*, which means "foam."

A DIFFERENT BIRTH STORY

Some Greek myths tell the same story in different ways. Aphrodite's creation story is a perfect example of this. According to some Greek myths, Aphrodite did not come from sea foam. These stories state that her parents were Zeus and Dione. Dione was a Titan goddess—one of the first gods created by Gaia and Uranus, the gods of the earth and the sky. Her name is the female version of Dios, a form of the name Zeus. Although Zeus was married to Hera, some myths say Dione was Zeus's first wife.

The Greek poet Homer passed this version of Aphrodite's origins down to future generations of Greek people. He lived around the same time as Hesiod. Through their stories, Aphrodite and the other Greek gods eventually became known throughout the world.

Zeus and Dione

GODDESS FACT

Because of the myths in which Aphrodite is said to be the daughter of Dione, Aphrodite is sometimes called Dionaea, a form of her mother's name.

The Origins of Aphrodite

Although different cultures have similar gods and goddesses, each one is a bit different. Aphrodite is part of the Greek **pantheon**. But similar forms of the goddess also exist in other cultures. Aphrodite is also identified with the Phoenician goddess Astarte, the Babylonian goddess Ishtar, and the Egyptian goddess Isis. Astarte was also her culture's goddess of heaven and war.

Aphrodite is different from the other goddesses found in the Mediterranean, though. She rules mainly over love.

pantheon—all the gods of a particular mythology

Egyptian goddess Isis

Chapter 3

APHRODITE AND HER FAMILY

Aphrodite had no full brothers or sisters. But as the daughter of Zeus she had many half-siblings. They included her half-brothers Apollo, Ares, and Hermes. She also had several half-sisters, including Artemis, Athena, and Persephone.

Ancient Greece was a much different place than the world is today. Among the gods in Greek mythology, many brothers and sisters had romantic relationships. This was the case for Aphrodite and Ares. But Aphrodite was already the wife of Hephaistos, the god of fire. Much like her father and many other gods, Aphrodite was often unfaithful to her spouse.

Aphrodite and Ares

14

When Hephaistos found out that Aphrodite and Ares had fallen in love, he made a plan to catch them together. He made it look like he was leaving on a journey. He then hid while he waited for Ares to come to Aphrodite. As soon as he did, Hephaistos dropped a large net on the pair. It trapped them so the other gods and goddess could see what Aphrodite and Ares had done.

Hephaistos hoped the other gods and goddesses would shame the couple. But Aphrodite's beauty was so great that at least one god defended them. Hermes, the messenger god, admitted to everyone that he would do anything to win the love of the stunning goddess.

When the other gods saw Aphrodite's affair with Ares, Aphrodite was embarrassed. But Poseidon, the god of the sea, comforted her. The two soon fell in love. They had a daughter together named Rhodos. She became the goddess of the island of Rhodes.

Hermes

GODDESS FACT

Hermes fell in love with Aphrodite too. It led to their child, Hermaphroditus.

APHRODITE'S MANY CHILDREN

The Greek goddess of love had more than a dozen children. Several of them were the result of her relationship with Ares. Their sons, Phobos and Deimos, often went to war alongside their father. Phobos was the god of fear. Deimos was the god of terror. Their talents helped Ares get the advantage even before the battles began. Their daughter, Harmonia, was the goddess of harmony. She was the opposite of Eris, the goddess of strife and discord.

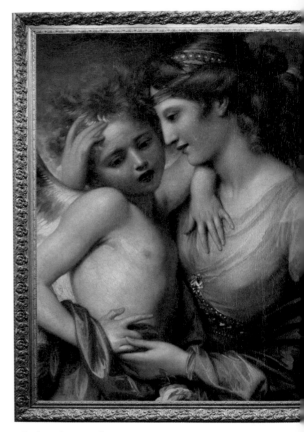

Aphrodite and one of the Erotes

Aphrodite is often pictured with one or more of the Erotes around her. The Erotes were winged gods and goddesses of love. In some myths, Aphrodite is called their mother. Of the Erotes, Eros was the god of passion. His twin, Himeros, was the god of desire. Pothos was the god of longing. Their other brother Anteros was the god of mutual love.

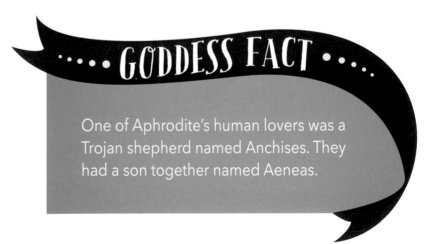

GODDESS FACT

One of Aphrodite's human lovers was a Trojan shepherd named Anchises. They had a son together named Aeneas.

Aphrodite and Adonis

Aphrodite was drawn to beautiful people. As soon as she saw the handsome infant Adonis, she decided he was meant to be hers. She hid him in a chest and asked Persephone to look after him. But when Persephone looked at the baby, she wanted him for herself. She refused to return him to her half-sister.

Aphrodite and Persephone argued about the matter until Zeus finally stepped in. He asked a **muse** named Calliope to decide the child's fate. Calliope declared that Adonis would spend half of each year with Aphrodite and the other half with Persephone.

muse—goddess of song, poetry, arts, and science in Greek mythology

Aphrodite's family tree

The goddess of love and beauty had many relationships and many children. Aphrodite's own birth myths have a couple different versions that add even more possible family ties. Her family tree shows some of the important connections Aphrodite had to other gods and even humans.

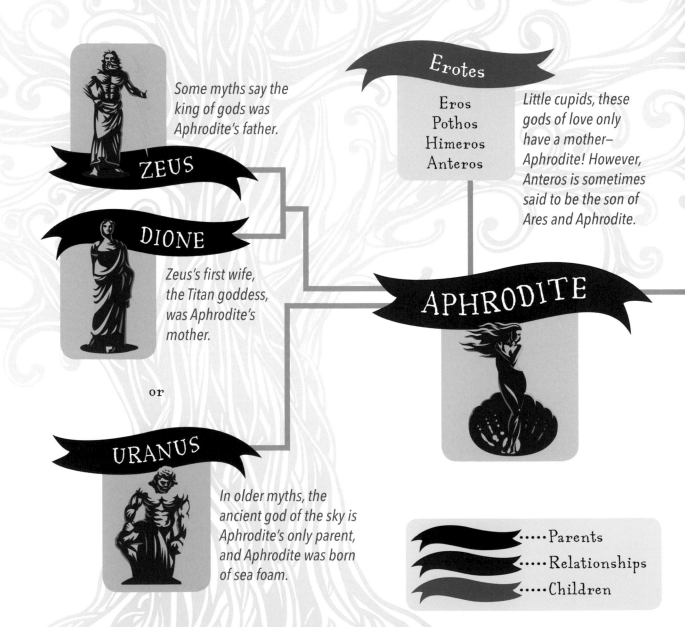

ZEUS

Some myths say the king of gods was Aphrodite's father.

DIONE

Zeus's first wife, the Titan goddess, was Aphrodite's mother.

or

URANUS

In older myths, the ancient god of the sky is Aphrodite's only parent, and Aphrodite was born of sea foam.

Erotes

Eros
Pothos
Himeros
Anteros

Little cupids, these gods of love only have a mother– Aphrodite! However, Anteros is sometimes said to be the son of Ares and Aphrodite.

APHRODITE

·····Parents
·····Relationships
·····Children

Aphrodite's husband was the god of fire. They had no children together.

HEPHAISTOS

Aphrodite had two sons with the god of war. Phobos and Deimos were the gods of fear and terror. Their daughter Harmonia was the goddess of harmony.

ARES

Phobos

Deimos

Harmonia

The messenger god had one son with Aphrodite. Hermaphroditus looked similar to the winged Erotes.

HERMES

Hermaphroditus

POSEIDON

Rhodos

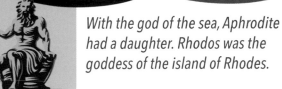

With the god of the sea, Aphrodite had a daughter. Rhodos was the goddess of the island of Rhodes.

Aphrodite loved a human man, and together they had a son. Aeneas became a hero of the Trojan War.

ANCHISES

Aeneas

Chapter 4

APHRODITE'S POWERS AND WEAKNESSES

Like all gods, Aphrodite was immortal. She also had the ability to inspire love wherever she went. Gods and men alike couldn't help but fall in love with Aphrodite because of her great beauty. But she was also capable of making gods and mortals fall in love with one another. Aphrodite could make the ordinary seem spectacular.

Aphrodite was known for having a magic girdle. This piece of clothing was said to make everyone desire the goddess. In one myth Hera borrowed the girdle to get the romantic attention of Zeus. The girdle inspires love and desire for its owner.

GODDESS FACT

In one myth, Aphrodite's magic girdle was stolen by Helen's servant.

Hera borrows Aphrodite's magic girdle. Sometimes she borrowed it to give to others to help stop married couples from fighting.

The ancient Greeks often looked to Aphrodite for help with their love lives. They wanted to feel special. And they knew she had the power to make that happen. Young brides asked her to help to make their weddings happy occasions. They also thought she could help their new marriages go well.

In some ways Aphrodite was even more powerful than Zeus. Although he was the king of all the gods, she led him into many of his love affairs with humans. Her power to affect Zeus's emotions angered him. He was also embarrassed when the other gods laughed at him for having relationships with humans. The gods saw themselves as better than people. In one myth Zeus got revenge on Aphrodite by forcing her to fall in love with the human Anchises.

Aphrodite falls in love with Anchises while he herds cattle. Dressed beautifully, she claimed to be a mortal princess. Aphrodite made even the animals she saw fall in love with each other.

APHRODITE'S DOWNFALL

Aphrodite's beauty and powers made her one of the mightiest goddesses. But like the other gods, she had her share of faults. One of them was her **vanity**. It was not just others who saw Aphrodite as the most beautiful goddess. She began to see herself that way, too, as was natural for her. Worse, she focused too much on what her looks could get her.

Aphrodite thought that she deserved everything and everyone she wanted. She was jealous of anyone who was also seen as attractive. And when she did not get her way, she became **vengeful**. Although she had the ability to inspire love, she spent much of her time causing others pain and discontent.

vanity—extreme pride in one's appearance or achievements
vengeful—wanting revenge

Aphrodite was often shown with mirrors to represent her vanity.

One of the ways Aphrodite hurt others was through her disloyalty. She fell in love quickly and often. Many times she chose the next object of her affection while she was still involved with another god or man. Many of them knew that she was unlikely to be faithful. But her immense beauty made them think she was worth the trouble.

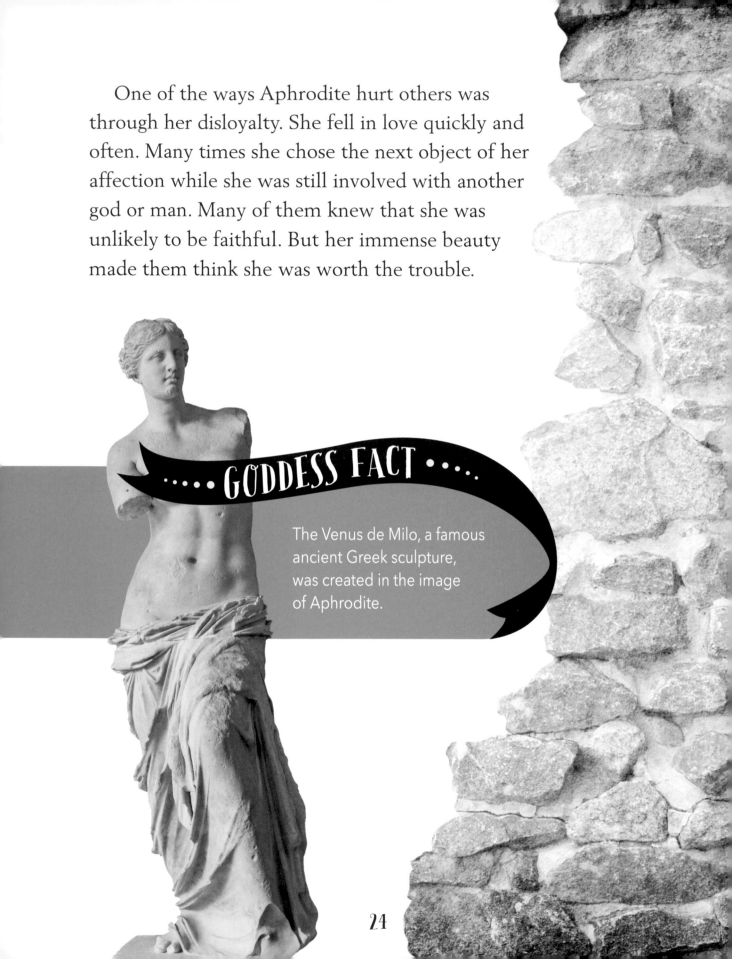

·····• GODDESS FACT •·····

The Venus de Milo, a famous ancient Greek sculpture, was created in the image of Aphrodite.

24

What Did Aphrodite Look Like?

Like the other Greek gods and goddesses, Aphrodite looked like a human. The ancient Greeks saw her as the ideal female. She was the highest symbol of physical beauty.

Artwork of Aphrodite usually showed her as a young woman. She had **delicate** features and was always smiling. In many paintings and statues, Aphrodite was nude. But she was also shown in elegant robes and jewelry.

delicate—small and fine

Chapter 5

APHRODITE IN GREEK HISTORY AND MODERN CULTURE

Ancient myths about Aphrodite linked her to Cyprus. This island played a large role in her origin story. Many ancient Greeks also believed that this was where the goddess lived when she spent time on Earth. Festivals were held on the island in honor of the love goddess.

Cyprus is an island in the Mediterranean Sea.

For many years stories of Aphrodite and the other Greek gods were passed down by word of mouth. Homer was the man credited with playing a large part in shaping their stories. He told these stories in the *Iliad* and the *Odyssey*. These poems from the 700s BC explain Aphrodite's origin. They also tell how the goddess of love became the wife of Hephaistos and the lover of Ares. Aphrodite came to stand for much more than beauty among both the Greeks and Romans. She also became a symbol of the passion and creativity that often goes with love. This image focused much more on the positive aspects of the goddess than the negative ones.

A 17th century artist's depiction of the poet Homer

···· GODDESS FACT ····

The Roman poet Lucretius called the goddess Genetrix. This mother figure stood for the spring, birth, and creativity.

APHRODITE'S MODERN FOLLOWERS

Aphrodite remains a major symbol of love and beauty in modern Greece and around the world. She is known far beyond the borders of her native land. The temple built for her on Cyprus has stood in ruins for more than 2,100 years. But people still travel to this famous site. Some even leave offerings for Aphrodite—just like the ancient Greeks did thousands of years ago.

The myths that brought Aphrodite to life for the ancient Greeks are also still told throughout the world. Stories about her even appear in modern fiction, such as Rick Riordan's *Percy Jackson* book series. Whether she is called Aphrodite or Venus, the goddess of love will truly live forever.

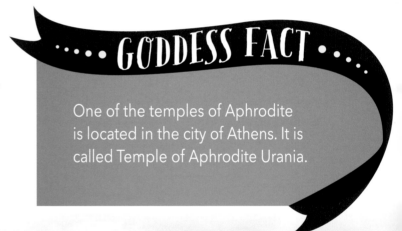

GODDESS FACT

One of the temples of Aphrodite is located in the city of Athens. It is called Temple of Aphrodite Urania.

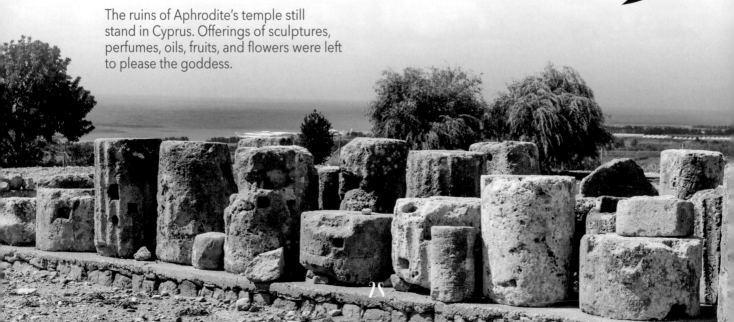

The ruins of Aphrodite's temple still stand in Cyprus. Offerings of sculptures, perfumes, oils, fruits, and flowers were left to please the goddess.

SYMBOLS OF APHRODITE

one of the Erotes

Aphrodite

doves, sacred animals

chariot pulled by doves

Did That Really Happen?

Most myths include some fantastic events. Humans have never seen many of the things that take place in these stories. Picturing Aphrodite being born from foam floating on water requires imagination.

Many people in ancient Greece believed myths were true stories. Some people today also believed these events really happened. But others see them as stories created to teach lessons. Whichever is the case, Greek mythology remains an important part of Greek culture to the present day.

An ancient water pitcher shows a scene from the myth known as the Judgement of Paris.

GLOSSARY

delicate (DEL-i-kit)—small and fine

discord (DISS-kord)—lack of agreement; conflict

generation (jen-uh-REY-shuhn)—a group of people born around the same time

immortal (i-MOR-tuhl)—able to live forever

mortal (MOR-tuhl)—human, referring to a being who will eventually die

muse (MYOOZ)—goddess of song, poetry, arts, and science in Greek mythology

nymph (NIMF)—a minor female goddess who lives on earth

pantheon (PAN-thee-on)—all the gods of a particular mythology

sickle (SIK-uhl)—a long, curved blade attached to a short handle

temple (TEM-puhl)—a building used for worship

vanity (VAN-i-tee)—extreme pride in one's appearance or achievements

vengeful (VENJ-fuhl)—wanting revenge

READ MORE

Braun, Eric. *Greek Myths*. Mythology Around the World. North Mankato, Minn.: Capstone Press, 2019.

Hamilton, Edith. *Mythology: Timeless Tales of Gods and Heroes*. New York: Black Dog & Leventhal Publishers, 2017.

Riordan, Rick. *Percy Jackson's Greek Gods*. Los Angeles: Disney-Hyperion, 2014.

Temple, Teri. *Aphrodite*. Gods and Goddesses of Ancient Greece. New York: AV2 by Weigl, 2016.

INTERNET SITES

Use FactHound to find Internet sites related to this book.

Visit *www.facthound.com*

Just type in 9781543554519 and go!

INDEX